LP

COUNTRY INSIGHTS
CZECH REPUBLIC

Rob Humphreys

RSVP

RAINTREE
STECK-VAUGHN
PUBLISHERS
The Steck-Vaughn Company

Austin, Texas

COUNTRY INSIGHTS

BRAZIL • CHINA • CUBA • CZECH REPUBLIC • DENMARK • FRANCE • INDIA • JAMAICA • JAPAN • KENYA • MEXICO • PAKISTAN

GUIDE TO THIS BOOK

 Besides telling you about the whole of the Czech Republic, this book looks closely at the city of Brno and the village of Nížkov.

 This city symbol will appear at the top of the page and information boxes each time the book discusses Brno.

 This rural symbol will appear each time the book discusses Nížkov.

Title page: Gabriela, Šárka, and Zdeněk at their home in Nížkov

Contents page: Hrad Castle looks down over Prague, the capital of the Czech Republic.

Published by Raintree Steck-Vaughn Publishers, an imprint of Steck-Vaughn Company

Library of Congress Cataloging-in-Publication Data
Humphreys, Rob.
Czech Republic / Rob Humphreys.
    p.   cm.—(Country insights)
    Includes bibliographical references and index.
    Summary: Introduces the geography, economics, and social structure of the Czech Republic, focusing on the city of Brno and the village of Nížkov.
    ISBN 0-8172-4795-5
    1. Czech Republic—Juvenile literature.
    [1. Czech Republic.]
    I. Title. II. Series.
    DB2011.H86   1998
    943.71—dc21   97-11623

Printed in Italy. Bound in the United States.
1 2 3 4 5 6 7 8 9 0 0 01 00 99 98 97

Contents

The Czech Republic

The Czech Republic is a small, landlocked country in the center of Europe. It is divided into two main provinces: Bohemia, to the west, and Moravia, to the east. The capital, Prague, lies at the center of Bohemia, on the banks of the Vltava River.

The Czechs are a Slavic people, whose ancestors settled in central and eastern Europe over 1,500 years ago. For many hundreds of years, the country was ruled over by the Austrian royal family. In 1918, the Czechs, along with their neighbors, the Slovaks, formed a new republic called Czechoslovakia. In 1948, a communist government took over Czechoslovakia, and the Czechs lost control over their own affairs. Communist rule lasted until 1989, and the country became very poor during this time.

◀ **This view over Prague shows the white church of St. Vavřinec in the foreground.**

4

This book will ▶ take you to the city of Brno and the village of Nížkov. You can find these places on the map.

There have been great changes in the country since communism collapsed, in 1989. For the first time in many years, Czechs can now travel abroad freely, start their own private businesses, and choose their own government.

In 1993, Czechoslovakia split into two separate countries: the Czech Republic and Slovakia. Today, the Czech Republic is one of the richest and most successful of the old communist countries.

Charles Bridge, a fourteenth-century ▶ bridge across the Vltava River, in Prague, was built long before the age of automobiles. Now it is a fashionable tourist attraction as well as a route for people on their way to work.

CZECH REPUBLIC FACTS	
Total land area:	30,260 sq. mi.
Population:	10.3 million
Language:	Czech
Capital city:	Prague
Highest mountain:	Sněžka, 5,256 ft.
Currency:	Česká koruna

THE CITY OF BRNO

Brno is the second-largest city in the Czech Republic. Its name is pronounced "Br-no"—the "o" is short as in the word "hot." The city lies in the southeast of the country and is the capital of the province of Moravia.

Only 200 years ago, Brno was still a small town with about 20,000 people who lived mainly inside the old city walls. The town's landmark has always been the cathedral, with its needle-thin spires.

BRNO FACTS

Population:	388,511
Height above sea level:	732 ft.

▼ *Behind the spire of the church of St. Jakub, you can see the high-rise apartments of Brno's suburbs in the far distance.*

The old medieval walls were taken down in 1860 and replaced by parks, gardens, and a ring road. At that time, Brno quickly began to grow into a big, industrial city, surrounded by textile and manufacturing factories.

In the 1960s and 1970s, Brno grew much larger, with lots of high-rise housing built in the new suburbs of the city. These apartment buildings are the first things you see as you enter the city. The old town is still in the city center, which has many cobbled streets and squares and several old churches. Only taxis and streetcars are allowed to move around the central streets of the old town. This is where most people do their shopping, and the vegetable market, held in one of the old town squares, is very popular.

▲ *Shopping at the vegetable market in the old town*

Brno's place in the Czech Republic

THE VILLAGE OF NÍŽKOV

Nížkov, pronounced "Neeshkoff," is a small farming village in the uplands of the Czech Republic, which stretch across the middle of the country from north to south. These gently rolling hills, known as the *vrchovina*, form the border between the two regions of Bohemia and Moravia. Over the last 100 years, all the traditional wooden houses in Nížkov have been replaced by brick and stone buildings. The oldest building in the village is the church, which was built some 700 years ago. The village also has a post office, a school, a bar, and three stores. The nearest railroad station is 2 mi. away on the main line from Brno to Prague, but only local trains stop there. There is no gas station, and although almost every family has a car, most people walk, bicycle, or use buses to get around.

NÍŽKOV FACTS	
Population of Nížkov and surrounding area:	805
Height above sea level:	1,726 ft.

▼ *The church of Nížkov, with its dome-shaped spire, is the highest point in the village. All the houses cluster below it.*

Unlike Brno, Nížkov has changed very little over the last fifty years. Roughly the same number of people live there, and farming is still the main activity. Although some young people leave to look for jobs in the neighboring towns or in other parts of the country, enough stay to keep the population from dropping.

The streets of ▶ *Nížkov are quiet and safe for these children to play in after school.*

Land and Climate

Two-thirds of the Czech Republic is forested, mostly with spruce, but also with pine and beech trees. Mountains form most of the country's natural borders. In 1945, after Germany had lost World War II, the 3 million German-speakers who lived in the border regions were driven out of the country. Even today, not many people live in these areas. Most Czechs live in the towns and cities in the flatter valleys of the Odra, Morava, and Elbe rivers.

The Czech Republic has four seasons. Winters, which last from November to March, are cold. Easterly winds from Siberia force the temperature well below freezing, and there are often heavy snowfalls in the hills and mountains.

▼ *Cows grazing in the rolling hills of North Bohemia.*

Summers are hot, especially on the flat plains of the Morava and Elbe rivers, with temperatures sometimes reaching 86° F. Spring and autumn are shorter seasons, with more moderate temperatures.

▲ *Skiing in the mountains of North Moravia*

The country has a lot of coal underground: brown coal (lignite) in North Bohemia, and black coal in North Moravia. Coal is the main source of energy, though the country also depends heavily on oil and gas imported from Russia. Acid rain is caused by pollution from the coal-fired power stations, and this rain has badly damaged the country's forests. The Czech Republic has one nuclear power station, in Moravia. It also generates some hydroelectricity from the dams on the Vltava River.

AVERAGE DAILY TEMPERATURE IN PRAGUE		
Winter (Jan):	Min.:	23° F
	Max.:	32° F
Summer (July):	Min.:	57° F
	Max.:	77° F

▼ **These thick pine forests are in the north, on the border with Poland.**

11

BRNO'S LAND AND CLIMATE

Brno lies on the border between the hilly uplands to the northwest and the flat plains to the southeast. The city center is built around two hills. The Gothic cathedral of Saint Peter and Saint Paul sits on the smaller hill, and the Špilberk fortress occupies the taller hill. On a clear day, you can see as far as the hills around Mikulov, a town 31 mi. to the south, near the Austrian border.

Many of the city's new suburbs were once small villages in their own right; these have since been swallowed up by the city. The outer suburbs in the north and west of the city have forests and hills at their doorstep. They are all within easy reach of the city center by streetcar or bus.

▼ *If you stand on the hill by the Špilberk fortress, this is the view of Brno that you see.*

Although the winters in Brno are cold and often bring snow, summers are hot with plenty of sunshine. The flat plains to the south of the city are especially good for growing fruits such as cherries, apricots, and grapes. Most of the country's wine is produced in the vineyards to the south of Brno.

Just beyond the city limits to the north is the Moravian karst region. Karst landscapes are made of limestone that has been worn away by rainwater to form underground rivers, lakes, and caves. The karst region is one of the most popular tourist attractions in Moravia.

You can take a boat ride to explore these ▶ underground caves, which are in the karst region just north of Brno.

NÍŽKOV'S LAND AND CLIMATE

Nížkov lies on a small tributary of the Sázava River, which flows west into the Vltava River, just south of Prague. In the uplands around Nížkov, the climate is generally much cooler than in Brno. The cherry, apple, and rowan trees, which line the country roads, blossom slightly later here. In winter, the snows are much deeper and the temperature can drop to as low as –13° F. Children in Nížkov learn to ski when they are young, as this is often the best way to get around in the winter.

▲ A map of Nížkov and the surrounding villages, made by schoolchildren from the village.

▼ Autumn leaves fall earlier in Nížkov than in Brno, because the village is on higher land.

The uplands have always been one of the Czech Republic's poorest regions. The soil is not very fertile and is only really good for growing potatoes and barley. Wheat and rye are grown, but the quality is poor. Smaller quantities of other crops are also grown in the local farms, including rape seed, peas, oats, beets, caraway seeds, and corn (which can be made into feed for animals). Many villagers fish for carp in the nearby freshwater ponds.

It rains the most in June, July, and August. August marks the beginning of the harvest, the busiest time of the year for any farming community. Just about everyone, young and old, lends a hand in the fields during this season.

"I like the farming life, especially the fresh air, the smell of the fruit, the meadows in blossom, and the birds."
—Bohuslav Hais, farmer (below)

◀ Bohuslav Hais prepares cabbage before it is taken to the village store to be sold.

15

Home Life

Family life is very important in the Czech Republic, and several generations often live together. Most Czech families have two children. Grandparents often look after the children while their parents are at work.

Czech homes vary greatly. In some parts of the countryside, people still live in traditional, timber-framed houses; in town and city suburbs, there are modern, high-rise apartment buildings, called *paneláky* (meaning prefabricated).

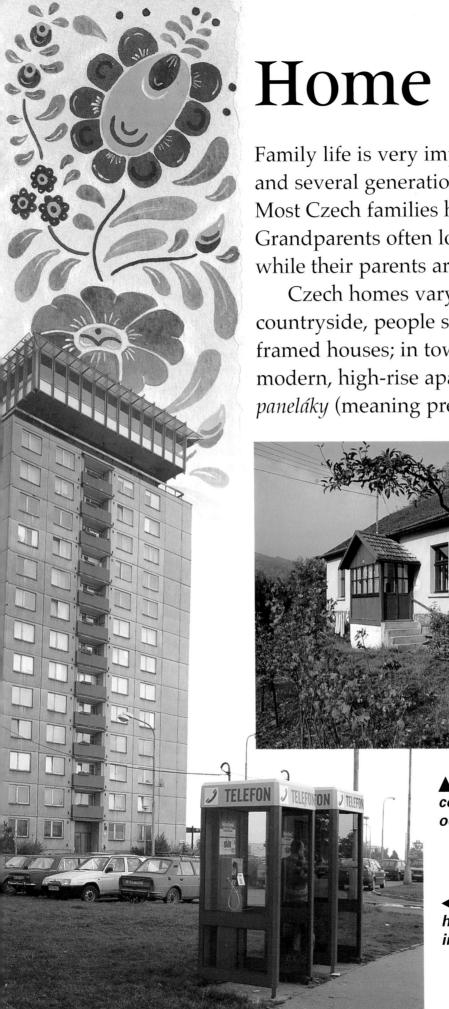

▲ **This big farmhouse in the countryside outside Brno is occupied by just one family.**

◀ **Paneláky,** *like this one,* **house hundreds of families in the Czech Republic.**

To save space, many Czech homes have special beds that can be turned into sofas during the day. Czechs usually take their shoes off when they go indoors and put on slippers known as *pantofle*. Visitors are also expected to take off their shoes and are given *pantofle* to wear by the family.

Most Czechs eat their main meal of the day at lunchtime. Lunch usually begins with soup, followed by a main course of meat with potatoes or dumplings. Czech dumplings are made with flour and milk and then cut into thick slices, rather like bread.

In the evening, the meal usually consists of cold meats, cheese, and bread, served with tea or coffee. It is really more of a snack, followed by chocolate, cookies, or an apple. Many Czechs have a sweet tooth and enjoy cakes and ice cream at any time of the day.

FAVORITE FOODS

Smažený sýr
(pronounced "Smadjeny-seer")
A thick slice of Czech cheese, deep-fried in batter and served with potatoes and tartar sauce.

Palačinky
(pronounced "Pala-chinky")
This is most Czech children's favorite dessert—pancakes filled with fruit or chocolate and cream.

Párek
A type of hot dog: a boiled sausage served with mustard and a white roll.

HOME LIFE IN BRNO

In Brno, as in all big towns, people live in many types of houses and apartments, from high-rise *paneláky* to luxury villas. The *paneláky* are mainly in the city's outer suburbs, and have been built over the last fifty years. Although these apartments have central heating and modern fittings, many of them were badly built and they often need repairing.

In the inner suburbs, there are two- or three-story houses, some with their own yards. Many of these used to belong to wealthy Germans before the end of the World War II.

In 1948, these and all but the

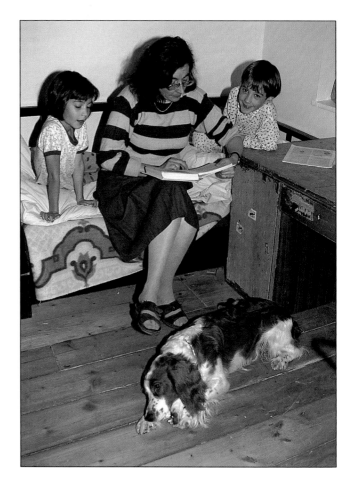

▲ *A Czech mother reads a story to her children at bedtime.*

◄ *Most people in Brno live in apartments; few have their own yards.*

smallest of other houses were divided into apartments after the communists took over the country. As a result, most people in Brno live in apartments, with one or two bedrooms, a kitchen, a bathroom, and a living room. Many apartment buildings have central courtyards with balconies overlooking them.

Most homes in Brno and other Czech cities have hot water and central heating, and most have a television set and a washing machine. However, computers, videos, stereos, and other high-tech gadgets are less common in Czech homes.

There are lots of different places to buy food in Brno, and most people don't have far to go to get to the nearest store. Apart from the popular vegetable market in the city center, there are also various supermarkets and smaller food stores around the city and its suburbs.

"We like getting take-out food some evenings, instead of having to cook."—Andrea and Tomáš, students at Brno University

HOME LIFE IN NÍŽKOV

◀ *Karel Novotný's, single-story house, which he built in the center of Nížkov for his family.*

There are no *paneláky* in Nížkov and few houses compared to Brno. Most families own their own houses, which are usually built on one or two floors and surrounded by a small plot of land. Villagers use this to grow their own vegetables and to keep a few hens and geese.

▲ *The Novotný family relaxes in the evening and talks about the events of the day.*

Nížkov is a very quiet village where everyone knows everyone else. Apart from the tractors from the local farms, traffic is very light, since most people do not use their cars much during the week. There is a regular bus service to the nearest big town, Žďár nad Sázavou, about 8 mi. away.

Karel Novotný is a truck driver and lives with his wife and three children. He delivers frozen meat and vegetables from Nížkov to stores all over the Czech Republic. His wife, Jana, has a part-time job delivering newspapers. She finishes work in time to take care of the children after school and to make the evening meal. Jana's ten-year-old daughter, Šárka, helps her mother clean, wash the dishes, and do the shopping.

Jana's parents also live in Nížkov. Her father used to work at a factory in Žďár nad Sázavou. He retired ten years ago, and now he gets a state pension. Jana's mother still works part-time as a teacher in the village school.

▼ *The evening meal is often the only time the whole family eats together.*

Work

For over 100 years, the Czechs have relied on heavy industries such as steel, coal, and manufacturing. The country has exported trains, cars, and, more recently, nuclear reactors to the rest of Europe. It has also equipped their armies. Since 1989, however, these old-fashioned heavy industries have found it difficult to keep up with the rest of Europe. The working people are well educated and highly skilled, but the technology used in the country is out-of-date. Many factories have had to lay off workers and cut down production. Others have had to close down completely.

▼ *This fertilizer factory will have to bring its technology up-to-date in order to survive.*

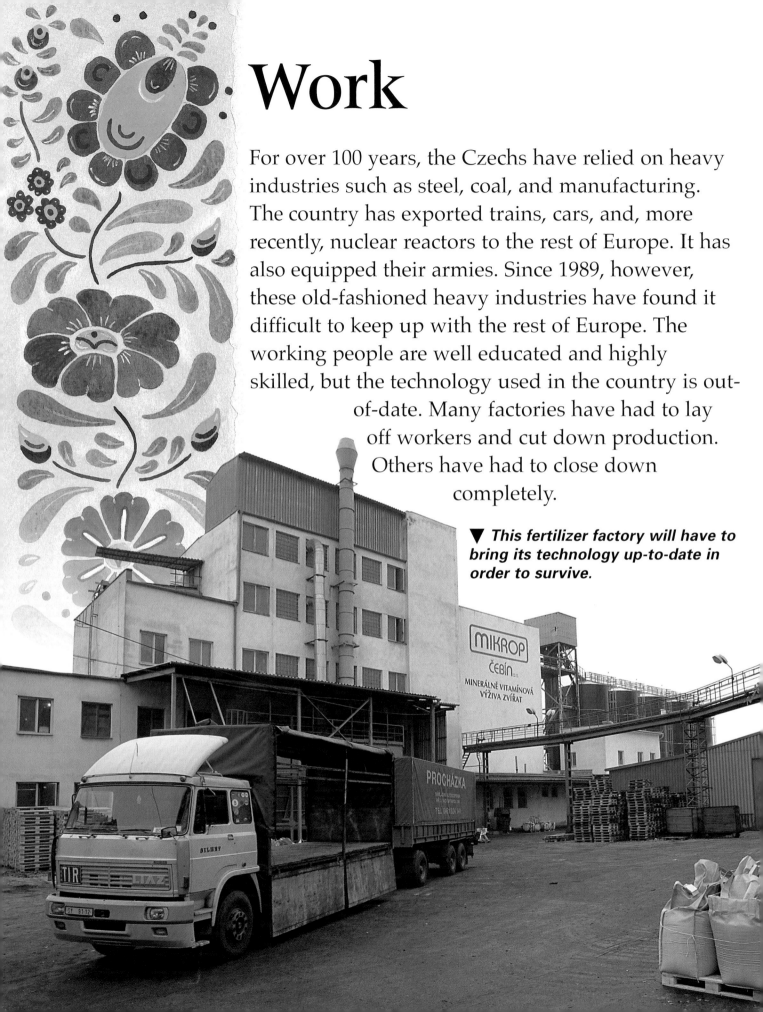

Under the communists, everyone was guaranteed a job for life—in fact, it was against the law not to have a job. Unemployment came as a shock to many Czechs.

TYPES OF WORK	Percentage of working population
Industry	42
Services	44
Agriculture	8

Luckily, most of those who were unemployed have now found jobs in the thousands of new companies that have started up since 1989.

Now that it is a lot easier to visit the Czech Republic, tourism has become one of the country's most important industries, especially in Prague. In 1995, more than 50 million tourists visited the country. This has created many new jobs for people who want to work in hotels and restaurants. There are also new jobs making consumer goods, such as television sets and CD-players. Other people work in computer technology, advertising, and the leisure and service industries.

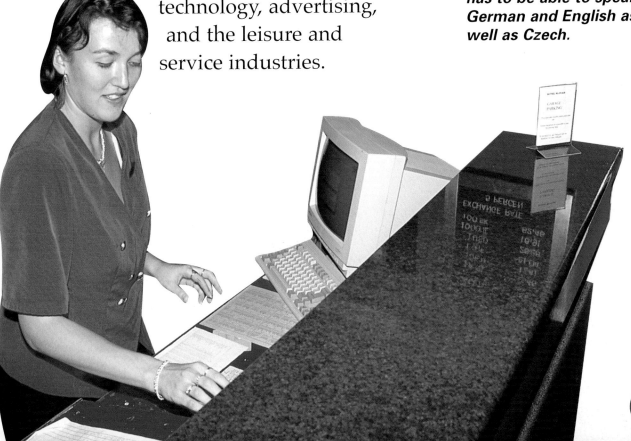

▼ *This woman works as a hotel receptionist. She has to be able to speak German and English as well as Czech.*

WORK IN BRNO

Brno is a center for textiles and manufacturing. It is also the agricultural center for South Moravia, where most of the country's wine is produced.

The city's international trade fairs are very important in central Europe, and businesspeople from all over the world go to them. The biggest one is the International Engineering Trade Fair, which takes place every year in September. There are other fairs throughout the year. Lots of people come to these fairs, which usually last for a few days. This provides good business for the city's hotels, stores, and restaurants.

▼ *A businessman makes arrangements to attend an important trade fair in Brno.*

▼ **Brno was one of the first Czech cities to get a new fleet of modern streetcars.**

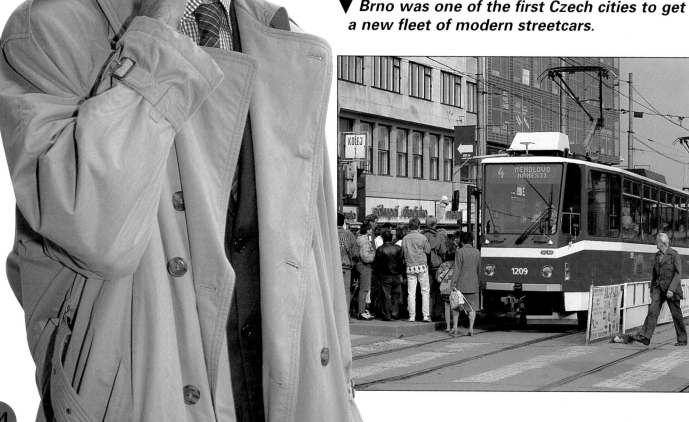

Most Czechs get up early in the morning for work. Many people in Brno use the city's public transportation system to get to their workplace. Factory workers, like Alena Černá, have to get up very early to be at work by 6:00 A.M. But since Alena finishes at 2:00 P.M., she has plenty of time to go shopping in the afternoon and prepare the evening meal for her family. All stores and offices close at 5:00 or 6:00 P.M., and open only until 1:00 P.M. on Saturdays.

People who are self-employed often work very long hours. Tomáš Novák runs his own newsstand and has to work from 8:00 A.M. until 7:00 P.M. Lenka Svobodová is an interpreter, translating for businesspeople at trade fairs. She works for herself and usually has more days off than most workers, but when she works, she often has to work right through the day until late in the evening.

**"I enjoy my work very much, and I meet a lot of people, but sometimes I have to work very long hours."
—Lenka Svobodová, interpreter (right)**

25

WORK IN NÍŽKOV

Throughout the communist period, most villagers in Nížkov worked in the area's big cooperative farm. Wages were low, but workers were paid all year round and were secure in their jobs. After 1989, the cooperative farm was divided up into much smaller private farms. Many of these farms are now run by single families, who can only take on extra workers at harvest time.

Ladislav and Zdena Pospíšil, who are both in their fifties, are typical local farmers. Their children have chosen not to follow the family tradition of farming, but they help out during harvest time. Ladislav and Zdena get up at 4:00 A.M. to feed the cattle, and work in the fields until it gets dark. They also raise rabbits, hens, ducks, geese, and pigs.

Ladislav and Zdena Pospíšil run their farm on their own for most of the year.

"The busiest time for all farmers is from June until early November. We work up to 14 hours a day, unless it rains very hard."—Ladislav Pospíšil, farmer

Some people work in the village's three stores, in the school, or in the post office. Several new businesses have started up since 1989. The largest one is a construction company, which employs many workers who build and decorate houses. Other new businesses in the village include a blacksmith's, a dressmaker's, a hairdresser's, and a plumber's.

▲ Workmen insulate a house to protect it from the cold and wet of winter. For the last five years, there has been plenty of building work in the village.

Some villagers have to travel to work in the nearby town of Žďár nad Sázavou, which has a large factory that makes machine tools. Factory workers have to catch a bus from the village at 5:00 A.M. to get to work by 6:00 A.M.

▼ At work in the village post office

Going to School

All Czech children between the ages of six and fifteen must go to school. Most begin nursery school when they are three or four. They then go on to "basic school," or *základní škola*, at the age of six and stay there until they are fifteen. Each class has one teacher for all subjects in the first four or five years. Then they have a different teacher for each subject. In the larger cities, there are schools that specialize in one subject, for example, science, languages, woodwork, or sports.

Children are given school reports twice a year, at the end of January and at the end of June. There are also exams at the end of June. If a child fails to do well enough in any subject, he or she may have to repeat the whole year.

◀ *This boy is learning carpentry skills in a school that specializes in woodwork.*

▲ *A game of charades helps children in their English class at school.*

▲ Physical education is an important part of the school curriculum.

Czech children do not have to wear school uniforms. However, all children (and their teachers) must wear *pantofle* inside the school building, just as they do at home. When they arrive at school in the morning, the children go straight to the coatrooms to change out of their shoes and into their *pantofle*. The atmosphere inside the school is very quiet, and there is not much noise in the school corridors. The children do not go out into the playground during recess, but they can play with their friends inside. Outdoor activities and games take place in the afternoon, after classes are over.

SCHOOL IN BRNO

Brno has plenty of schools from nursery level right through to college. Seventeen-year-old Václav Cerný goes to a senior high school, which specializes in subjects like history, literature, and politics. He has to catch the streetcar to school at 7:30 A.M.

Václav's younger brother, ten-year-old Jan, goes to the basic school near their home. Like most pupils, Jan walks to school, where classes begin at 8:00 A.M. He carries his books on his back in a brightly colored schoolbag.

"School's okay, but my favorite class is PE, when I get to play soccer and other games."—Jan Cerný, age 10

Many children in Brno ▶ live close enough to school to walk there.

Jan has five or six different classes every day, with a short break after every one. Each class lasts for 45 minutes. Lunch is at 12:30 or 1:30 P.M., depending on the day.

After lunch, the school organizes outdoor activities and games. Children do not have to go to these if they prefer not to. Václav and Jan both go on at least one school field trip a month, to a museum, a theater, or some other event. There are nature trips, too. Every spring, there is a weeklong school trip to the mountains of North Moravia. There are not enough places on these trips for all the children to go, so they must take turns.

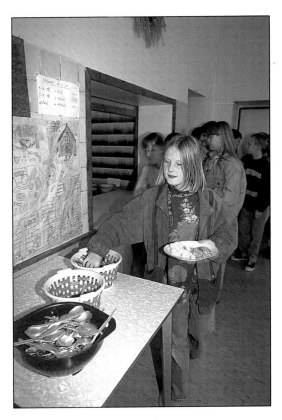

▲ Lunchtime in the school cafeteria. Children line up to be served a hot meal.

▼ A game of "Yes or No" in an English class, where the teacher says something in English, and the children race to the chair marked "yes" or the chair marked "no" depending on whether the statement is true or not.

SCHOOL IN NÍŽKOV

The main school in Nížkov is a basic school for children between six and fifteen years old. To go to senior high school, the children must travel to the nearby town of Žďár nad Sázavou. They catch the bus from Nížkov at 7:00 A.M. There is also a nursery school in Nížkov for children from three to six years old.

The basic school in Nížkov is quite small, with just 177 pupils and thirteen teachers. In Nížkov, school starts earlier than in Brno, at 7:15 A.M. Some children arrive even earlier and spend an hour in the school playgroup, or *družina*. Like most children from Nížkov, Šárka Novotná walks to school by herself or with her younger brother and sister.

▼ *These children are learning English at school in Nížkov.*

All three Novotný children have to get up very early in the morning in order to get to school on time.

Šárka has her lunch break at midday. The meal is served in the village nursery school, five minutes' walk away. Šárka likes the food at school except when it is spinach or soup.

The children are given a small amount of homework twice a week. Any children who do not do their homework are made to stay after school and do extra work. There are regular field trips to the movies and theater, and once a year the whole school goes on a day trip. Last year they went to the safari zoo.

▲ **Children on their way to school in Nížkov**

Šárka does her homework in her bedroom. ▼

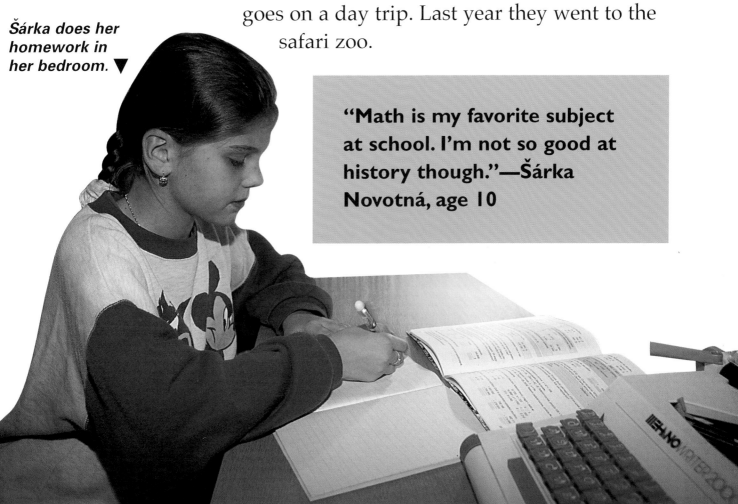

"**Math is my favorite subject at school. I'm not so good at history though.**"—**Šárka Novotná, age 10**

Leisure Time

Ice hockey and soccer are the most popular sports in the Czech Republic. Even the smallest towns and villages have a soccer team, and most large towns have a *zimní stadión* ("winter stadium"), where people play ice hockey. Sometimes, younger children practice ice hockey outside, using roller skates instead of ice skates.

Many Czechs love to go walking and camping. There are marked paths all over the country that make it easy for people to plan their walks. From an early age, many children go to organized summer camps, where they learn rock climbing and canoeing. In the evenings, they often sit around the campfire and sing popular folk songs, accompanied by the guitar.

Czechs are enthusiastic tourists at home and abroad. On weekends, many families visit nearby castles or museums and have picnics. Under the communists, very few Czechs were allowed to travel abroad for their vacations. Since 1989, however, bus tours to neighboring countries have become very popular.

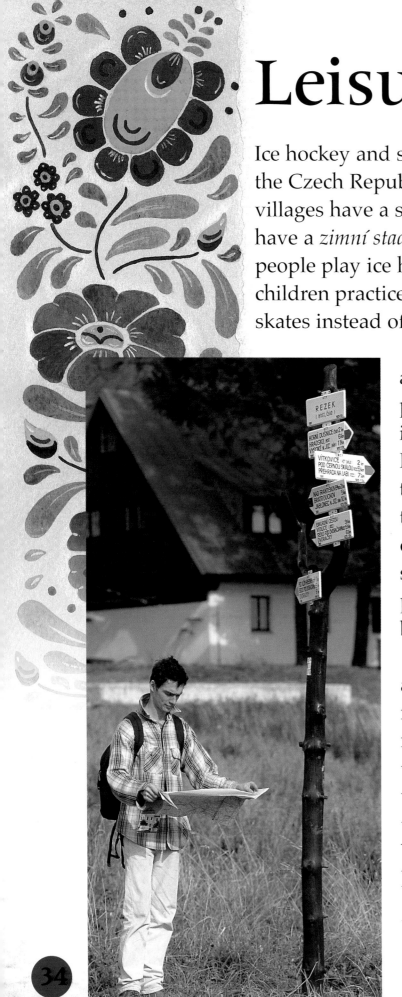

◀ *A walker plans his route in the Krkonoše National Park.*

34

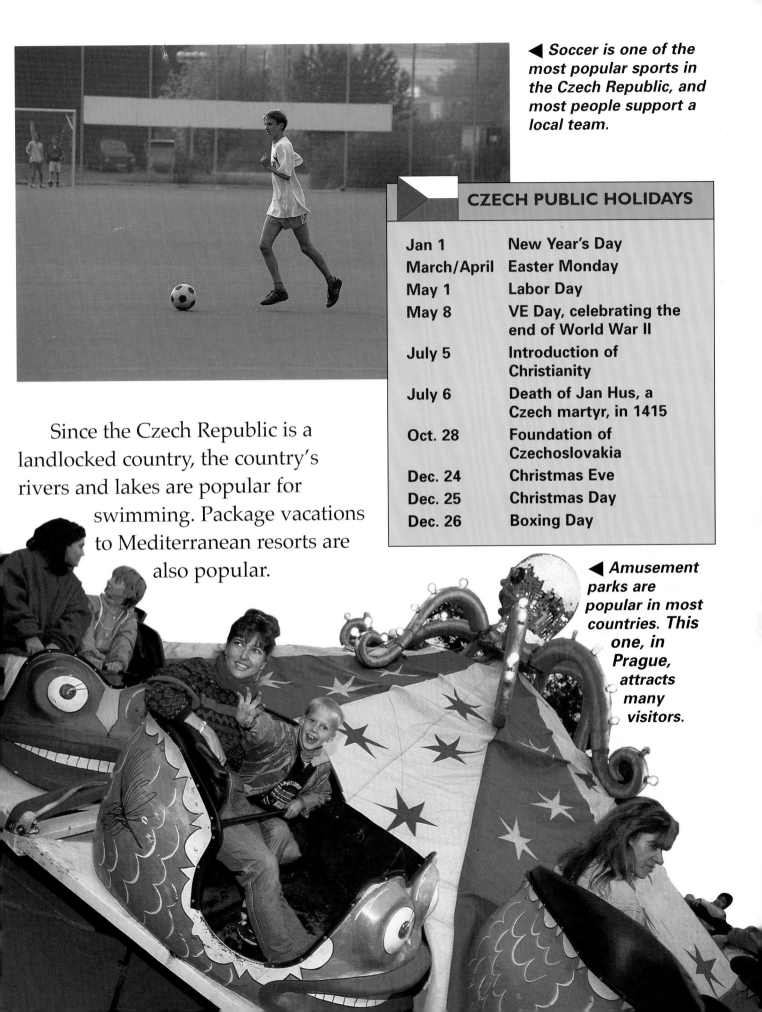

Soccer is one of the most popular sports in the Czech Republic, and most people support a local team.

CZECH PUBLIC HOLIDAYS

Jan 1	New Year's Day
March/April	Easter Monday
May 1	Labor Day
May 8	VE Day, celebrating the end of World War II
July 5	Introduction of Christianity
July 6	Death of Jan Hus, a Czech martyr, in 1415
Oct. 28	Foundation of Czechoslovakia
Dec. 24	Christmas Eve
Dec. 25	Christmas Day
Dec. 26	Boxing Day

Since the Czech Republic is a landlocked country, the country's rivers and lakes are popular for swimming. Package vacations to Mediterranean resorts are also popular.

Amusement parks are popular in most countries. This one, in Prague, attracts many visitors.

LEISURE TIME IN BRNO

Most families in Brno like to get out of the city on weekends. Many families own their own *chata*, or have friends who do. A *chata* can be anything from a small piece of land with a simple wooden hut on it to a much larger country cottage. There people from cities can enjoy cleaner country air, grow their own vegetables, or simply relax with friends. Even those people who do not have a *chata* to go to usually head out into the country for the day if the weather is good. There are forests and hills to the north and west of Brno, just a short streetcar ride from the city center.

▼ *Czech families who are lucky enough to have a* chata *can escape from the city on weekends.*

Children in Brno playing ▶ in the school gymnasium after school

"We have a television at home, but I prefer to go out and play sports with my friends after school."—Eva Kriatková, age 13

▼ *Brno's new sports stadium, one of the city's popular leisure facilities*

There are many more leisure facilities in Brno now than there were ten years ago. Next to the soccer and ice-hockey stadiums, there is now a new entertainment complex. It has a multiscreen cinema, gymnasium, pool hall, bowling alley, and roller-skating rink. The city also has a Grand Prix circuit, which hosts an international motorcycling race every August.

Young people have several movie theaters, dance clubs, and music clubs to go to, though most international bands perform only in Prague. Older people sometimes prefer to go to the theater or to the opera. Tickets are inexpensive, and people like to get dressed up to go there.

LEISURE TIME IN NÍŽKOV

Life in Nížkov is much quieter than in Brno, and sometimes the only sound in the evening is the chiming of the village church clock. Every house in the village has television, but many children prefer to spend their free time outside with their friends. After school, Šárka Novotná likes to play *prehazovaná*, a popular game similar to volleyball.

As farmers, Ladislav and Zdena Pospíšil do not have very much free time. Ladislav usually watches the television news in the evening, but once a week he goes to the local bar to play cards. The bar serves hot food throughout the day.

People who want to visit a restaurant or see a movie must drive or catch the bus to Žďár nad Sázavou.

Children in Nížkov have lots of opportunities to enjoy outdoor life. There are freshwater ponds nearby where they can go fishing. The hills surrounding Nížkov are good for walking, and in winter there is usually plenty of snow for skiing.

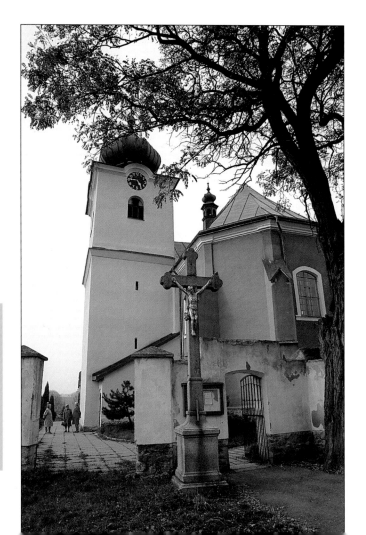

▼ *The church plays an important part in the life of Nížkov, but nowadays it is mainly older people who go there.*

"*Prehazovaná* is my favorite game, but I also like swimming in the summer."
—Šárka Novotná, age 10

At Christmas, the focus is on children. On the evening of December 5, three villagers disguise themselves as Saint Nicholas, the Devil, and an Angel. They stop at each house, threatening to give naughty children coal, before finally giving them presents for being good. On Christmas Eve, the children open presents from their family and friends. Carp is the traditional Christmas dish, taken fresh from the local fishponds and kept alive in the bathtub until it is cooked and eaten.

▼ *Nižkov schoolchildren have lots of opportunities for getting out into the country. These children are on a school field trip.*

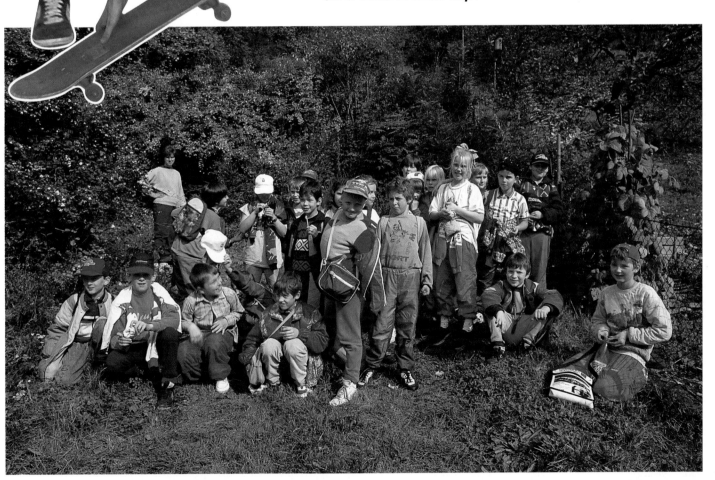

The Future

The future for the Czech Republic is much better than it was under communist rule. Now that the country is a democracy, people are free to express their opinions, travel abroad, start their own businesses, and write and read what they like. None of these things were allowed under communist rule.

However, there is a lot of work to be done as the country adjusts to its new government. The Czech Republic needs help from other countries to bring its industry up-to-date and to create jobs for the unemployed.

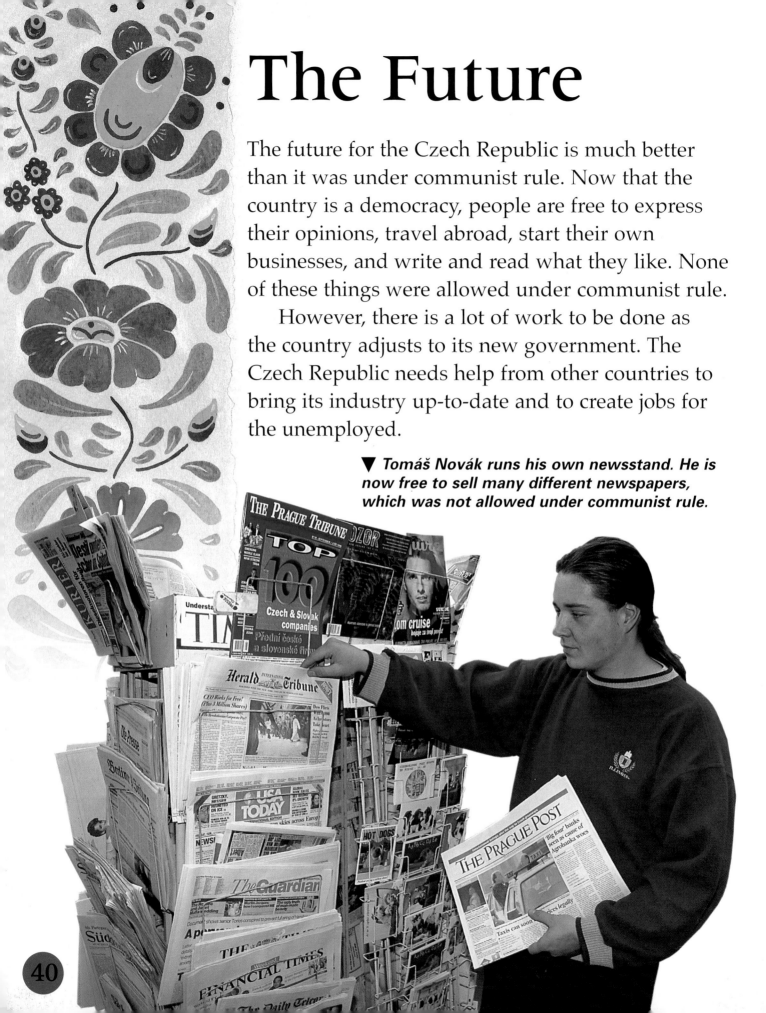

▼ *Tomáš Novák runs his own newsstand. He is now free to sell many different newspapers, which was not allowed under communist rule.*

The biggest problem facing the country is the pollution caused by the coal-fired power stations, which creates a permament smog over parts of the country, particularly North Bohemia. Nuclear power produces 29 percent of the country's electricity, but some people think it is dangerous. The country needs to look for other sources of energy, such as solar power and wind power, which cause less pollution.

The Czech Republic can solve these problems in time. In fact, the country hopes to join the European Union (EU) early in the next century. So far, it is the one country in Eastern Europe that seems likely to do this.

▲ *Tourism is a growing industry in the Czech Republic. New hotels like this one will create wealth and employment.*

▼ *Smokestacks like these create a lot of pollution in Czech towns and cities.*

THE FUTURE OF BRNO

More people can ▶ *afford cars these days, so there is much more traffic in Brno today than there was a few years ago. This often causes traffic jams and congestion.*

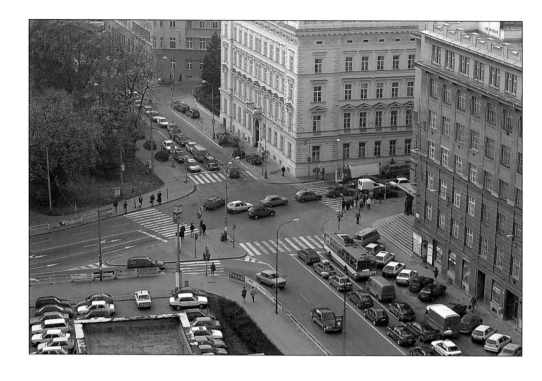

Brno's problems are typical of the country as a whole. It makes its money from heavy industries. These industries are now producing less and employing fewer workers. Many big factories have been taken over by companies from Germany, Italy, and the United States. This has kept them from being closed down completely, so the number of people who have lost their jobs is much smaller than people feared. In fact, unemployment in Brno is only half that of the national average. As they grow, new businesses help keep unemployment low by taking on more workers. There are new stores, cafés, and restaurants all over the city center.

"At one time it looked as though all the city's factories were going to close down. The fact that they are still in business at all is a success of sorts."
—Alena Cerná, factory worker

There is much more traffic in Brno today than in 1989. Although public transportation is more expensive than it was, prices are still kept low with money from the government. This is to encourage people to use the streetcars and buses rather than their cars. Trains are improving, too. A new high-speed railroad is planned to link Brno with Prague and with Berlin, in Germany, and Vienna, in Austria.

The city's trade fairs have become even more important since 1989, creating jobs for many people and increasing business at the city's hotels, stores, and restaurants. Brno's trade fairs have also allowed foreign businesspeople to meet with their Czech partners. Czechs have been very good at getting foreign companies to put money into the country, but Prague often gets the larger part of this new money.

▼ Waiting for a streetcar. Cheap fares encourage people to use streetcars, which cause less pollution than cars.

▼ Foreign investors talk business at a Brno trade fair.

THE FUTURE OF NÍŽKOV

When the communist government was in power, the local cooperative farm employed most of the villagers in Nížkov. The government provided money to keep the farm going, and there was always work and enough food. Life in the village did not change much over the years. However, the farming methods were not up-to-date, and people had no reason to work more than was absolutely necessary.

Since 1989, many people have got back the land that the communists took from them. Farmers can now work for themselves and their families. They know that if they work hard, their farm will do well, and they will make more money.

▼ *Farmers like Ladislav Pospíšil have to work even harder than before, because they no longer get help from the government.*

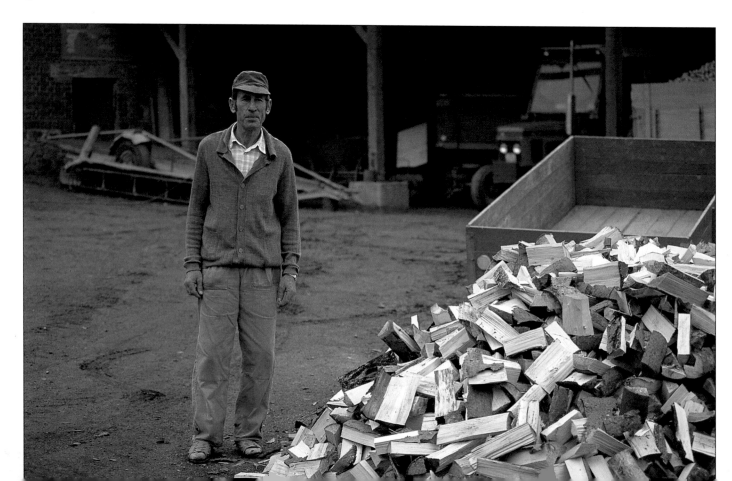

The government no longer gives the farmers any money to help them, so life is much harder than before. But the village still has a strong sense of community, so people are happy to help one another through these difficult years of change.

Like most villages, Nížkov's biggest problem is trying to keep its young people from leaving. There is not much choice of work in the village, and the farmwork is usually seasonal. However, there is more opportunity now for starting small businesses, and several are doing very well. There are also jobs at the nearby factory in Žďár nad Sázavou. This factory is doing well thanks to new orders from less economically developed countries, such as Pakistan.

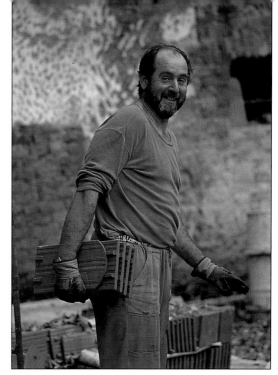

▲ *This builder has become successful by starting his own business in Nížkov. Small businesses will be very important to villagers in the future.*

"I think there is a better standard of living now than under the communists, with more choice in the stores and more opportunities for my children."—Jana Novotná, villager

The children of Nížkov will ▶ *have easier lives than their parents have had.*

Glossary

Acid rain Rain containing acid that kills trees and plants. The acid comes from waste from factories.

Ancestors People from whom we are descended.

Boxing Day A holiday marked by giving "Christmas boxes" to service workers.

Chata A Czech word for a small country cottage.

Communist government A type of government where everything is owned and controlled by the state, instead of being privately owned. A communist government ruled Czechoslovakia from 1948 until 1989.

Cooperative A business run by the workers themselves, with everyone sharing the profits.

Democracy A system of government that lets people vote for any political party they want to.

Gothic A style of building popular from the twelfth to the sixteenth centuries; it featured pointed arches and tall spires.

Heavy industries Industries such as steel and manufacturing, which make large items such as machinery for factories and cars.

High-rise housing Tall apartment buildings that can house many families.

Hydroelectricity Electricity produced from the power of water.

Interpreter Someone who translates speech from one language to another.

Landlocked Having no coastline or access to the sea.

Medieval From the Middle Ages, A.D. 600–1500.

Prefabricated Made by putting together ready-made sections.

Provinces Regions of a country.

Republic A type of government without a king, queen, emperor, or empress, usually headed by an elected president and a parliament.

Ring road A road that goes around the outside of a town, to keep traffic out of the center.

Self-employed Running one's own business.

Service industry Businesses such as tourism and banking, which do not make goods but instead supply people with services they need.

Slavs A group of people who come from the central and eastern part of Europe.

Solar power Energy from the sun.

Suburbs Outer parts of a town or city where people live.

Trade fair A big meeting of business-people where they can buy and sell their products.

Translating Changing a word or sentence from one language into another.

Tributary A river or stream that flows into a bigger river.

Uplands A mainly flat area on the top of a range of hills.

Further Information

Books to Read

Burke, Patrick. *Eastern Europe*. Country Fact Files. Austin, TX: Raintree Steck-Vaughn, 1997.

Mayberry, Jodine. *Eastern Europeans*. Recent American Immigrants. Danbury, CT: Franklin Watts, 1991.

McLeish, Ewan. *Europe*. Continents. Austin, TX: Raintree Steck-Vaughn, 1997.

Rohr, Janelle. *Eastern Europe: Opposing Viewpoints*. San Diego: Greenhaven Press, 1990.

Symynkywicz, Jeffrey. *Vaclav Havel & the Velvet Revolution*. People in Focus. Parsippany, NJ: Silver Burdett Press, 1995.

Useful Addresses

Czech Republic Tourist Office
10 East 40th Street
New York, NY 10016
(212) 689-9720

Czech Embasssy
3900 Spring of Freedom Street
Washington, DC 20008
(202) 363-6315

Picture Acknowledgments

All photographs except the following, are by Dorian Shaw, of Axiom Photographic Agency: Page 11(top): Image Bank; page 13 (bottom): Robert Harding Picture Library.

All map artwork is by Hardlines.
Border artwork is by Kate Davenport.

Index

Page numbers in **bold** refer to photographs.